You Never Know

poetry

Chris Anderson

STEPHEN F. AUSTIN STATE UNIVERSITY PRESS

Stephen F. Austin State University Press
PO Box 13007, SFA Station,
Nacogdoches, Texas 75962.
sfapress@sfasu.edu

Book Design by: Emily Townsend
Cover Design by: Emily Townsend
With permission, cover art by: Jim B. Janknegt, "Walking on Water"
www.bcartfarm.com.

ISBN: 978-1-62288-209-0
First Edition

for my father
Wayne Anderson
1931-2017

Contents

You Never Know

All those countless centuries
before I was born it wasn't so bad.
I didn't feel a thing.

Is this what it's like when we die?
Do we just cease to exist?

Or do the angels fly out to greet us,
skimming over the bright green fields?

You never know.

When I had breakfast at Fairwinds Spokane,
Spokane's premier luxury
retirement community,
the old women in their flowery blouses
and the men in their motorized chairs
chatted and laughed at the dining room tables
like kids in a school cafeteria,

and the sun streaked through the windows,
and the oatmeal steamed in our bowls,
and even my hunched
and befuddled father was smiling
for a moment, almost coherent.

I couldn't have been
more surprised: how happy I was.

Desire

I catch a glimpse of a face, a cheek,
a curve of hair. But what I feel isn't desire.
It's admiration. When I wake up

the power is out and the house is cold
and driving into town I see a bucket truck
and men in hard hats
slinging a line, and I'm filled with gratitude.

You just have to stand still,
let your eyes go soft, and wait.
That warbler you heard: a branch will bob.

A leaf.

That's it.

The Mercy Seat

When I tipped Timmy's crib into the trench
at the landfill, a bulldozer simply
rolled by and flattened it. Kept going.
But I've never forgotten that moment.
The golden cherubim on either end of the lid
that covers the Ark of the Covenant
reaching towards each other, wings almost
touching. There the Lord will come
to meet us, and from above the Mercy Seat,
from between the two cherubim,
in the space beneath those golden wings,
he will deliver all his commands.

It Won't Be Long Now

I waltz into the room and shape an arabesque.
Pirouette. Perform my sensitivity.

But popularity never lasts,
not here or anywhere else.

In 2034, according to the Vatican Astronomer,
an asteroid the size of the English Department
will smash into the earth, and all our plans
that day will come to naught.

We are chatting over tea at the palace.
Scones and clotted cream.
Bougainvillea blooms in the papal gardens.

It's like when you're walking down the stairs
and you think, hey, I'm walking
down the stairs, and suddenly the rise and fall
of your own two feet seems entirely
improbable. Completely crazy.

It won't be long now, says the monkey,
as he backs into the lawnmower.

The Neskowin Cottage Walk

Montaigne was fifty-nine when he died. Not even
sixty. But I'm feeling fine, walking through one beach house
after another at the annual Neskowin Cottage Walk.
I love looking at other peoples' houses. The soft couches
and the shelves with their books and all the touching signs
of habitation. A coffee pot. A toaster. A vase of flowers
on a window sill. Why should we fear dying? Once
Montaigne was thrown from his horse. He raved and tore at
his doublet. But inside he felt *a pleasure in gently letting go . . .*
an infinite sweetness in repose. The smell of salt air.
The sound of waves crashing beyond the dunes, coming in
and going out. *The fact is,* he says, *I was not there at all.*

Christmas Letter

It's the morning of Christmas Eve and I'm painting the bathroom.
I just started. I'm trying to figure out how to maneuver in there
with the paint and the ladder and the trays. How best to reach the ceiling.
Foggy outside, but the sun coming through. This is the morning

we decided to put our cat down, too, and I've been thinking about that
as I soak the roller and begin to smooth the paint on the wall.
She was a little squirrel of a cat, dust-bunny gray, furtive and unmannered,
and I'm checking in with myself to see if maybe we've behaved callously

in taking her to the vet this morning, Christmas Eve of all days,
when the Child was born in a manger among the cows and the sheep,
with their sweet, warm breath. But it feels right to me, though sad.
This power we all have, of life and death. These choices we all make.

When I look back on the year I realize that more and more the events
of my life are interior. Nothing much seems to happen. But it does.
In secret. In silence. *All that is asked of each of us is to wrestle in faith
with God and with whatever opposes us in the world*, Guardini says.

In the Christmas letter I got the other day from an old friend
in high school, someone I always looked up to and used to think of
as very smart, as a genius, he misspells the word *empirical*, talking about
his cats and dogs and grandkids—he spells it with an "I"—*impirical*—

and that really surprises me and bothers me, though of course
empirical is a good word for talking about the realism we need to have
as we grow older, the facing of facts, the giving up of illusions,
and in any event forgiveness is the most important thing of all,

compassion, first towards ourselves, and then towards others—
towards all living things, all that moves and breathes and has its being.
And I rub and I roll, and the roller squeaks, and the walls smooth out,
a greenish-blue this time, clean and bright for another few years.

How solemn painting is, how formal: the careful preparations,
the spreading of cloths, the small, deliberate movements of hands.
There's a kind of quiet at the center. A kind of tenderness.
Things have been stripped away. Things are about to change.

I Think I Hear the Cry of Geese

I keep thinking I'll get over these feelings,
my anger, my fear. How sitting around a table
I don't really love anyone. But no.

These are the feelings I am called to have,
all of them. This is what I am being given to feel.

Stepping out on the porch I think I hear
the cry of geese in the morning sky. But it's
just my neighbor up the hill, calling in her dogs,
softly, babytalking. Winter. Cold and dark.

What I don't understand at first
is her babbling. Her quiet voice, like a mother's.

How She Loves Me

for Sister Teresa

The morning moon through the bare
branches of the maple, and I think of Mary

reflecting the light of her son. Black sky
with stars and the forest still black. What's left
of the snow on the cold, cold ground.

Silence. Stillness.

And the moon is full and bright
and white as shell, and the light that falls
falls on everyone. O Lady,

how you love me. How you love us all.

The Unexamined Life

Floating on a broad river of sadness.
Through a gorge. Bright sun.
Not consolation or desolation but something else.
The way I was in high school
when every morning I woke up joyous
and just did things and everything was easy
but now the joy is so thinned out
and sheer it's more like detachment.
The philodendron snips I keep
putting in little vases with nothing
but water and somehow they keep growing.
They're all over the house.
I think about them. I keep track of them.
And the fog in the morning and how
it slowly burns off as the day goes on.
Leaves. Stars. Sometimes
the unexamined life is worth living.

Outlet

A kitchen outlet didn't work so I replaced it,
and when that didn't work we called an electrician,
and when he couldn't draw the power in
he started looking for where the problem was.
He kept going up into the attic, and down, waving
a meter. You sure don't have a problem with insulation,
he said through his mask, his gray hair flecked
with fiberglass. At first he thought the power drain
was behind a cupboard where the oven used to be,
but when he wrestled the cupboard out, carefully,
inch by inch, trying not to split the façade,
that wasn't it. By now over an hour had gone by
and it was dinnertime. Time and a half. A nice man,
in his fifties, with a sick wife at home. Premier Electric.
So he went up into the attic again, crawling
through the thick, smothering layers, waving his meter,
and when he came down he said, *there*, behind
the bookcases in the living room, I think it's there,
and I knew then what I had to do. I started pulling off
the books that I'd arranged so carefully over time
and tossing them in piles, then sliding back the cases,
first one, then another, until at last, behind
the shelves in the center where I'd lined up, by size,
the books that I most loved, Gilbert and Berry,
Stafford, Brooks and Warren, we found the source,
the half-melted plug, black with what had once been fire—
on the back of the shelves the scorch marks,
wide and sooty and dark, like the shadow of a hand.

The Big Parade

Gulls blown in by the storm circle a college dumpster.
Gray, windy skies. Gulls and the cries of gulls, here in the valley,
sixty miles from shore. The kiting of gulls.

Come, my soul, says Father de Caussade, let us abandon ourselves
purely and entirely to God's design, without all these fears
and reflections, without all these twistings and turnings
and disquietudes. Let us pass with head erect over all that happens
within us or outside us, remaining always content with God.

The night before the big parade I jump out of bed
and start putting on my uniform, my North Central High School
marching band uniform, scarlet and black and cream.
I'm buttoning up my brilliant blouse. I'm squaring up my epaulets.
Come, my soul, let us vault over all this earthly labyrinth!

And then I hear my father's voice, calling down the stairs.
No, son! No. It's not time. *You're still asleep. You're still asleep.*

Take and Read

I thought the sign on the door of the tavern
said *No Mirrors Allowed*.
I accepted this. Lots of things were mysteries.
I thought the man on top of Old Smokey
had lost his poor lover for *recording too slow*.
This made sense to me, and it still does.
When Augustine flung himself down
under the fig tree, and he heard the voices
saying *take and read, take and read*,
he changed his life, he decided to believe,
even though he knew
these were just the voices of children
playing beyond the garden wall.
Ashes! Ashes! All fall down!

How Warm They Were

The mother was holding the baby in her arms,
and she was rocking back and forth, and she was wailing,
the sound of it came in waves, rising and falling,
and I came into that room, and I said the words,
and they were beautiful words, and they rose and fell,
too, they had a rhythm and a force, and I think
after a while they started to calm and center the people
in the room, as I said them into the dark air.
But mostly what I felt was helpless, was powerless,
and I *was* helpless. I was powerless. It was the words
that mattered, and what was deeper than words,
I could feel it—I wasn't thinking about myself at all—
for a moment I was caught up with the mother
and the father and all the aunts who were wailing
and the grandmothers and the grandfathers
and all the people in the world in that terrible,
beautiful darkness. "Let the children come to me,"
Jesus said. "The kingdom of God belongs
to such as these." And He was there, in the darkness.
Jesus was there. I can't explain it. At the end,
as I made the sign of the cross on the baby's forehead,
as I touched her cold, lifeless skin, I could feel
the tears of the mother falling on the back of my hand.
How warm they were. Almost scalding.

Hangman Creek

I didn't know where we lived with grandma in the little house
under the bridge was called *Peaceful Valley*.
All the shabby houses. The raggedy pine. I didn't know
we were poor. Mom said there was a fat lady at the corner store

who used to sell us penny candy and that she cried
when we moved away, but all I remember is the honeysuckle
we sucked on the steep, brambly bank above. I didn't know
anybody loved us. I didn't know a creek flowed

behind the little house, and still does, not a hundred yards away,
so stern were my mother's warnings, so blindly did I obey.
Over rocks, then down, beneath the complicated black scaffolds
of the bridge, where even further back, the story goes,

they once hung an Indian from a tree. *A horse thief*,
Mom said. *A bad man*. I didn't know. Everything has a name.

Malta

In Malta we dug a hole in the earth
not far from the banks of the Milk River,
deep enough for two of us to stand in
and wide enough for two of us to sit in,
then roofed it over with leafy cottonwood branches
and hid out and waited.
The pleasure of not having to get anything straight.
The firmness of the earth. Also the sweetness.
How the mosquitoes swarmed and bit
as soon as we got out of the car fifty years later,
the river nothing more then than a muddy trickle,
seeping around small islands of brush.
That dusty little town on the Highline.
Miles and miles of nothing but miles and miles.
But what I want to say
is that as we crouched beneath the striped
and stippled shade of the branches
happy and sheltered and snug,
through the dark walls of the earth
and the sweetness of the earth and the firmness
we could feel the river flowing
just beyond us, we knew it was there,
strong and milky and deep,
and we still do.

So Long to Remember

I dug ditches for Mr. Willmering,
whose wife was ugly, but kind.

When my brother came to dig ditches, too,
she made us tuna sandwiches
in her clean, white kitchen.

Why does it take so long to remember?
Why does it take so long to heal?

Carl Sandburg was a terrible poet,
a professor once told us—he said this
waving his hand—and it's taken me
forty years to get over it.

Shoulders of hills. Stalks of corn.

Rich loam of the earth
where we buried the pipe.
Sweet smell of the earth.

The Divine Milieu

Some books I won't even open.
They just sit on the shelf,
gleaming.

God bless you please,
Mrs. Robinson.
Heaven holds a place
for those who pray.
Hey Hey Hey

Wipers beating. Summer rain.

Once, in our nation's capital,
I stood before a painting
so huge it took up a whole wall.

Great peaks. Shining water.
Tiny figures exactly my height
either coming or going.
Either morning or evening.

Litany of Praise for American Public Education

Thank God for desks in rows and books on shelves
and the alphabet scrolling above dusty chalkboards.
Thank God for Mrs. Chapman in her long, smooth skirts
and Mike Mars, X-15 pilot and Mike Mars, Astronaut
and Meg Murray in a *Wrinkle in Time*, her braces just like Kathy's.
For Alan and Dave and Shane. For Linda. For Cheryl.
Thank God for Waltzing Matilda, Waltzing Matilda,
you'll come a-waltzing Matilda with me. Thank God for words
in a line and words on a page and the whole system
of American public education, which taught me how to read
and taught me how to write and taught me how to throw a football
like any good American boy. Thank God for solar winds
and for the atom and the parts of the atom, and thank God
for the scientific method: phenomena, hypothesis, experimental
verification. And he sang as he watched and waited
till his billy boiled, you'll come a-waltzing Matilda with me.
Thank God for the glimpse I had through a window in the gym
of Megan peeling off her sweater, and thank God for the ponderosa
by the gym and the needles of the ponderosa and the piney smell
of the needles, and for the blue sky above us, and the clouds.
Thank God for the Madison Elementary Fall Carnival
and the booths and the lights and winning the Cake Walk
and walking Cindy Goble home through the dark
and standing on her front porch trying to tell her I liked her
while holding the cake with both hands. A white cake,
with vanilla frosting. O Mister Moon, moon,
bright and shiny moon, won't you please shine down on me?

Knowledge

Mary Ruth meets me on a hill
in a little cemetery among the trees
and leads me to the grave
where her boys are buried,
in a single coffin,
Willie on one end, Tom the other,
elbows touching.
They drowned, they pulled each other in,
1975. Now Mary Ruth is old,
and she is weeping,
and she keeps wiping her nose
on her faded sleeve.
A beautiful sunny morning, early fall.
I look out at the fields and farms
and everything is turning.
Everyone knows something.

How Traveling a Long Way is Like Dying

You forget all about the life
you thought you loved: your books. Your coffee pot.
The way in the morning the carpet feels
on your bare feet when you swing your legs out of bed.

You're just walking down a narrow stone street
with shops on either side and all you're thinking about
is spices. Saffron. Tahini. Also Roman coins,
watches, fabrics of many colors and designs.
You're brushing shoulders with many people, some
of them in headdresses. The men have dark beards
and are shouting and gesturing. It's wonderful.

It's like a tunnel and maybe when you come out
the sun is setting on the sea and you're eating a fish
someone just pulled out of the shining waters
and you can't believe how good it tastes.

And none of this is to any purpose.
It doesn't matter at all.

I should say that you're traveling when you're older
and you've finally accepted the fact
that you've done all you're going to do with your life.
You've accomplished all you're going to accomplish.
So you're not bringing any of this back
to impress anyone. The beautiful things
you're seeing are just for you. They're just inside you.

No one knows you in the dark churches.
No one knows you in the markets.
No one knows you.

One afternoon the guides let you off by the side
of a road and you walk a little way

into a small, narrow valley: smooth grassy slopes,
then rocky cliffs on either side.
Flowering mustard.
Other flowers you can't name.

It's late in the day and the shadows are gathering
and the air is cool and dry and the path
curves ahead slightly into some soft, green trees.
The last light is hitting the top of the cliffs.

The Valley of Doves, they call it,
because the doves nest there
in the cliffs and coo and mourn but also because
when the wind comes down through the gap
it sounds like doves and it sounds like sighing.

Jesus walked here, the guides tell you.

He must have.
It's the only way.

Another State

Lately I've felt these pockets of contentment.
I sit on the couch and look out the window.
The furnace kicks on. Slows. Quiets.

Wouldn't it be nice not to have to breathe anymore?
Just to give all that up?
The ins and the outs, the repetition.
And personality, too, the tedium of it,
and all the backlog of memory. The intricacy.

I'm coming home from the debate tournament
and I'm running out of gas.

It's the middle of the night.

I'm driving back from another state,
in my cherry red Impala, a 64, low and wide,
and I'm watching the needle go down
and Terry with her bare knees way over
on the passenger side, leaning
against the door. Pulling away in the dark.

I can barely see her. My old partner.
Pea coat backwards,
up to her shoulders. Eyes closed.

My cherry red Impala,
rumbling through the night
like a destroyer.

Liberty Says Hi

An old friend calls after forty years
and I wonder, who are we really,
when everything is stripped away?

Emerson had pie for breakfast.
Lincoln, too.

Apple or cherry or peach,
with thick, doughy crust.

Jesus is the Bread of Life.

The dragon waits to devour the child but
the child is born and the mother lees
and the child grows up to be human

like the rest of us. He tends his sheep
and thinks his thoughts.

And the name of the child is Liberty.
And the name of the dragon is Time.

Ephphatha

That night you came over to cook me dinner
you wore a poodle skirt.

I lived in the desert, then, in a cinderblock house.

I was a scientist, patches on the elbows
of my rumpled tweed.

The night was cool and clear,
and we went out on the patio to look at the stars,
and looking up, you said,
I've never seen the moon shaped like an egg,

when a giant meteor came flaming
over the ridge and slammed into the earth,
plowing a long, glassy furrow.

The ground rippled out in waves,
and for a moment there wasn't any sound,
and then all the Fiestaware
in the kitchen started to rattle,
bouncing up and down in its rickety racks.

The cinderblock began to glow.

Ephphatha! Jesus whispered: *Be opened!*

And I was.

Gemini 8

Sure I panicked when the thruster stuck.
Who wouldn't? The capsule started spinning.
The planet blurred: ocean, then space, then ocean.
The other guys grumbled when I got back,
but believe me, I never wanted to splash down.
The bright curve of the air. The dark swirl of a storm.
It was like when we were kids and Tim and I
started to fight. *Time for the gloves!* Dad would say,
lacing up our Everlasts. Then we'd knock
each other senseless. It was like I had no hands.

My Eagle Scout Ring

We only offend God when we do something
contrary to our own good, Aquinas said.
And we decide. We choose the darkness

or the light. A few years ago I would have
denied how good it was to come across
my old Eagle Scout ring again, in a box of

old, forgotten things: a silver band with
a silver eagle set against a red and blue shield.
But I was just trying to be a man. Thrifty

and brave. Or that day on Mount Spokane
spreading hay beneath the ski lift
and how sweet the air was and Alan and Terry

laughing and trying to throw handfuls
of hay at each other and the hay scattering
in the air and breaking up into stalks

and the stalks floating down on their faces,
and the air, the great gulf of the air, and
the world spread out before us, far below,

blue with distance, and the valleys,
and the valleys, and the valleys.

What We Weigh

There was a man who thought
the soul had weight,

so he put dying people on a scale and weighed them,
just before and after they died,

and what he found is that the instant people die
they are 21 grams lighter than they were before.

Exactly. Every time.

An enormous scale, a body on one side,
weights on the other.

Even a breeze could cause a wobble.

A mere breath, the man who stood so firm,
a mere shadow, the man passing by.

When the researchers set up the nets
between the trees, and caught the birds they caught,
behind us, in our forest,
they untangled each one, carefully, making sure
not to damage the wings—warblers and chickadees
and thrushes—they were wearing gloves as they did this,
but even then they could feel the beating
of those tiny hearts, and the warmth of those feathery bodies—
and then they weighed each bird, hanging it
by the feet from a small scale before letting it go.

The one I remember is a Wilson's Warbler,
a lovely pale yellow, with a jaunty black cap.

I closed it in my fist, but gently, hardly
crushing the feathers.

Then I opened my hand and it shot away,
a yellowy flash, back into the trees.

.27 ounces.

Sisters

Einstein's sister was a singer,
I learned last week.

And many other things, too, I'm sure.

Winter now, leaves falling from
the trees one at a time.

A young woman lifts the hem
of her long, green skirt
and trips lightly up the stairs.

Like a dancer. A queen.

Clutch

My first time in hell the monsters really scared me,
especially the people who kept changing into lizards
and back again. But the next trip I made them pets.
I slipped a leash around Geryon and suddenly he shrank.
His scorpion tail became plastic. They all still followed me
around, horns glinting, but every face looked like mine
in the fifth grade. The rivers of blood were just my arteries,
my veins. Gradually I began to feel very happy.
Sure, it smelled bad in hell, and there was all this wailing,
but I never paid much attention to the punishments,
to the whirlwinds and the hackings and the boiling pitch.
It was the levels I loved, the way the circles worked.
I laughed out loud in the Malebolge when I finally saw
how the pieces fit, and even Virgil smiled a little,
I think, like Dad the first time I didn't pop the clutch.

The Book of Love

After Deception Pass we drove to Cape Disappointment.
Waves crashed on the rocks below.

"The soul," you said, "is like a wild animal.
If you go shouting through the woods, it will run away.
You have to be very patient. Hold very still."

I said, "a comparison with the sea may also prove instructive."

"When a winter storm whips up the waves,
you can't tell where to cast your nets.
The wind must die and the water clear
before you can see all the way to the depths."

By then it had begun to rain. A fine, gray mist.
We were standing on the edge of the continent.

After a while you asked, "Who wrote the *Anima Christi*?"
"I don't know," I said. "Who wrote the Book of Love?"

Mike Mars Astronaut Wakes Up

Mike Mars astronaut is growing old
and his spirit flags.

In the morning he looks into the darkness and is afraid.

By the lake there were Golden-Crowned Kinglets
pecking in the lower branches,
their yellow-streaked heads like the helmets
of the Michigan Wolverines,
and the ice has melted away, and the trail
is clean now, and soft, but nothing finally
lifts the burden he feels.

The nose of the capsule spins up
and light floods the cabin.
How he loved those old metal switches
he could flip. Dials like the dials
at Diablo Dam, huge.

But those days are gone.
Fly-by-wire: he lacks the courage
for. O Lord, he is pointing
towards the moon, which he knows
is cold. Is there. Is hanging.

Is a real place.

Curves.

Change Position

A man comes to tell me this story. My age.
A general contractor. His hands at communion
like broken countertops.   Not long ago
he went back to his pew and kneeled to pray.
His eyes were closed. But he was in a different
part of church this time, he said.   It's good
to move around. You should tell people that.
So he was in a different part of church, to the side,
and his eyes were closed, and you know
how when your eyes are closed and someone shines
a bright light at you? You can see it, through
your eyelids? That's what it was like, there was
this bright light shining through my eyelids,
and I thought, wait? What's happening?
And when I opened my eyes and looked around
I saw the sun just peeking out from the window
on the opposite side, the sun was just rising,
topping the sill, and it was spilling into the pew,
it was slanting down, and I felt so warm and happy.
The light was so warm and bright. Golden.
You should tell people that: *change position.*

Brother Sun, Sister Moon

Sluggish and slow, all day an emptiness,
a grayness, and the Spirit doesn't move
and God doesn't exist, until I drag myself home
and reach into the cupboard and realize
I'd mixed up the canisters that morning,
I'd made decaffeinated coffee, the dark cups
had been a lie. O Lord! All praise for caffeine,
and all praise for the body, and all praise
for the hallucinogenic mold that furred the bread
that St. Francis ate before he walked out
into the beechy woods and preached to those
medieval birds, the starlings and the sparrows.
And they listened. I know they did.

Enlightenment

The man by the lake is tossing
a stick for his dog. I hate him. He's a faker,
I can tell already. Graying beard.

Slight paunch: get the fuck out of my woods!
I'm nothing like you. I will never die.
And fuck the woods, too! Fuck the woods!

I'm sick and tired of them, of the endless
repetition of the trees. Of all the circles
I seem to keep going in. When the hawk

looks down from the empty sky
I know what's it thinking:
Too big to eat and too heavy to fly.
What difference could he make to me?

My Soul, the Sea

I'm talking with a friend about God and about life,
and I've just said, it's like pushing on an open door,
something gives, when a woman pushes through the heavy,
glass door of the coffee shop, and the morning sun shines
through her hair, and for a moment I am in love with her,
with the softness of her face and the pursing of her lips.
How often I fall in love. Every day I fall in love
a hundred times. All the beautiful women in the world!
Their hands are like doves. Their thoughts are often
elsewhere. They are wearing long, lavender scarves,
and I pretend not to notice, but I do. I am standing at the door,
Jesus says, knocking, and he is. I have great confidence
in my masks. They are good masks, serviceable, tested
over time. But they are only masks, hard as candy,
and as brittle, too, and underneath them is whatever reality
is. Maybe an abyss. Maybe a vast cavern. Maybe a sky
with stars. I am pushing through an open door
and I am the door. My ego is a boat. My soul, the sea.

My Mother's Soap

Standing by the pond, looking
into the trees, I catch the sharp,

clean smell of my mother's soap.
Her Dove. Her Tide.

Could it be her?

Or is it just some chemical
released by the rain, something

in the leaves, or deep down
in the freshness of the pond?

Everything's better
when you've given up hope.

Mom Could You Have Known When in the Evening

Mom could you have known when in the evening
you played the Moonlight Sonata
on the piano in the living room
and I sat on the porch in the dark and listened
through the screen to the slow rise
and fall of the notes,
full of sadness and beauty and grief,
that one day after you were gone
I'd be listening to it again in a hotel room
by an airport and that I would rise up and look
at myself in the mirror and see the grim
tendons of my father?

A Question for the Stream

The winter rains have swelled the stream
and now a river roars beneath us, down

in the ravine where we never go,
surging and rushing through the trees.

But how can I let my heart leap up,
how can I love you, as I do,

when soon I know the rains will pass
and the waters cease to flow?

Washing Windows

Washing windows while listening to *The Sound of Music*.
Early fall. *Climb every mountain. Ford every stream.*
Sliding out the inner window, popping out the screens.
Humming. *When the dog bites, when the bee stings.*
I can't remember if it was my mother who taught me this
but I use newspaper for better absorption, bearing down
in smaller and smaller circles until the wad shreds
and the glass squeaks. The sharp, clean smell. The shining
of the glass and the trees coming through and the sun.
Doe, a deer, a female deer. Somewhere in my youth
and childhood. The minute I walked through the door
every day I knew the way she was. She wouldn't even turn.
But we all went to see *The Sound of Music*, in a theater,
and for weeks she played the album, over and over,
and I'd lie on our green shag listening to the French horns
and the twittering of the birds as the music begins to swell
and Julie Andrews twirls and twirls and the camera rushes up
to her creamy young face, and it was the mountains, too,
I was thinking of, and the brilliant green of the valleys,
and how precious and pure Julie was, and how she loved
all the children, even those ridiculous, sissy boys,
with their soft, white skin. How she taught them all to sing.

A Story in the Desert

Clark Gable is telling Marilyn Monroe
a story as he drives her through the desert
in a big, white station wagon, 1961.

This is in *The Misfits*, the last movie
either ever made. They both died not long
after, Marilyn face down on her bed,
after swallowing a bottle of pills.

Gable is a cowboy in the movie,
an aging, crinkly cowboy,
with a cocked hat and a look in his eye.
One hand on the wheel.

Everything is black and white.

"A city boy sees a country boy
rocking on his porch."

A sideways glance, at Marilyn.

"Can you tell me how to get back to town?
Nope.
Can you tell me how to get to a train?
Nope.
Can you tell me how to get to a road?
Nope.
You sure don't know much, do you?
Nope. But I ain't lost."

And Marilyn laughs. Nervously.
Uncertain. She is glowing like a pearl.
She is luminous. She is wearing
a scooped black dress with skinny straps
that keep falling from her wondrous,

blurry shoulders, but you don't want
to make love to her. It's not like that.

There's something about her mouth,
a softness, an indistinctness. She is
gradually coming apart, she is slowly
disappearing, and somehow you know this.

Outside the windows the desert
keeps going by. The rocks and hills.
The bare, dry earth. Beyond
the ridge the testing grounds, smooth

and bright as glass.

Slate Creek

Only our Fairlane on all the Colville Highway,
only the ribbon of road and the high grass giving
way as we move and everywhere
the fields and farms, and the hills and sky,
just these haystacks and just these barns,
as they always already are. It's we who are gliding.

Bumping along the logging roads on the way
to Slate Creek, only us in all
the forest and in the valley opening up
to the clattering stream and the meadow
where we make camp and build the fire and lying
out in the open look up at the impossible

field of stars and know,
exulting, exactly what those spaces mean.

Gemini 10

He was always the thumb at the finger party.
Then he left home and pushed the outside
of the envelope and the call came from Deke.
He stammered yes and his whole life
quickened: mockups and barrel rolls, blastoffs
and mission rules. The Big Blue Marble.
The Great Black Void. I can't get enough of this,
especially the sadness and the emptiness.
That the wind is not the sail. The fish is not the net.

Transfigurations

for Bob

When we climbed the Mount of Transfiguration
we didn't know your heart was failing.
You could have had a heart attack right there, at the top,
where we celebrated mass on that kind of patio
with the corrugated roof and Jesus may or may not have been
bathed in light. You were white as chalk. Short of breath.
I thought you were just tired. I was tired.
Remember all the garbage in the town at the foot of the hill?
The ugly little houses, square, dirty white?

For a moment today as they were cracking you open
and spreading back the layers I believed everything was true.
The bread really was the Bread.
The wine really was the Wine.
I didn't want to talk about it anymore or try to explain it.
It just was.

Do you remember the other Mount of Transfiguration,
on the way to the Golan Heights?
It could have happened there, too, at the source of the waters
of the Jordan. No one really knows.
I loved how smooth the water was as it curved over a shallow ledge.
Several caves rose up behind us and there was a high, grassy ridge,
but the water is what stays with me now,
and the coolness of the water,
and how clear and clean and simple it seemed. That glittering sheet.

Omniscience

I wish I could be omniscient, like the author of a novel
I read about an old man who on the outside
was cold and hard but on the inside was full of sorrow
and regret and who loved his children after all.

I'd like to understand my father,
if in his dark room he was hiding or in prayer.

The author of the novel was a friend, in fact, we taught
together for years, though once I saw him
in the hospital parking lot, from the back, and he'd grown
so thin and frail I didn't recognize him at first.

We said hello, and promised to meet, and now he is gone,
and he knows what he knows, and I know what I know, too.

The sorrow. The regret. The sun pouring down
on the parking lot, every windshield a star.

At Keats's Grave

The tombstone was shaped like a large, white thumb,
hard to get into the frame. The famous inscription read,
"Here lies a young English poet, whose name is writ in water,"
and standing there in Rome, at the Protestant Cemetery,

I thought of how young Keats really was, younger
than my sons. How he rose up at the end and cried out.
But I was exhilarated. I had this sense of being
on an expedition and of having found what I was looking for.

Of having reached my destination. The cemetery is walled,
and when you walk in through the front gate the graves
are thick on either side of a tree-lined lane. Keats's
is in the far corner, to the left. You turn, and in a few steps

the stones thin out and the trees thin out and there's a sense
of spaciousness. It's more like a park. And the trees, I started
to realize, had been reminding me of the trees in Spokane.
They were some kind of pine, and their needles on the grass

and their piney smell had been reminding me of Ponderosa.
Of the way things looked and the way things felt
when I was a boy, in the woods above the river. Of the wide
spaces between the trunks. The dark, volcanic rock.

Driving Back

When Randy and I drove his beat up camper
all the way to Montana,
into the bare, grassy hills, to a brown lake,
we just turned around
and drove back.

I drove and drove, all through the night,
until I thought I was seeing
deer jumping out
over the dark road, high in the air,
blurry white deer,
antlers like oaks.

A Blind Boy, on the Solstice

A blind boy whose father dies finds no comfort
in a picture of him standing by the roses.
The musk, maybe, of an old sweater he used to wear,
but that will fade. If only the boy had saved
a few of the voicemails his father was always leaving,
all the times and places they would meet.
We never know what we really need. Here, let me
take you down to the banks of the swollen river.
Let me take you to where the river has begun to flood.
Every winter at the solstice we walk among
the muddy leaves. Every winter at the solstice we listen
for the high thin notes of the kinglets foraging
in the upper branches of the oak, with the chickadees, too,
and the yellow-rumped warblers: *tsee tsee tsee.*
Their quick, sweet, tumbling chatter. I will teach you
what to listen for. You can count on this: the solstice
always comes and the kinglets always fuss,
high in the bare trees, and every winter the river floods,
it thickens and swells and increases in volume
and increases in force, sweeping up branches and trunks
and carrying them along. Let me try to describe it.
The river is rising now. It's beginning to race. It's thick
and brown and wide. If we wanted to keep up
we'd have to run, faster than we've ever run before.

The Exact

St. Isidore the Farmer used to pray at the plow
and the angels would follow along, squawking
above the furrows like gulls behind a tractor.

What else can we do, but live the lives
that we've been given? The leaves are sifting down
and the sun is pouring down and I am crossing
the quad again, my twenty-third fall, walking briskly,

and what I say now is blessed are you
when you are persecuted means blessed are you
when you don't care what people think.
We are given what we are given. We are made
for those we are made for--for this work and no other.

The ship that sailed into the harbor
was called *The Exact*, and the captain exulted
when he looked up from his maps:
The dark forest! The great, shining mountain!

The Creation of Light

foggy the morning I am about to teach
the parting of the waters,
the creation of light,

and a young woman in a wheelchair
paused at the curb,
arms flapping,

until a young man with a beard
dismounts
from his bike and stoops to retrieve
the bottle she's dropped

and can't reach
and can't reach

Daffodils

Mine are late again, just thin green spears
poking up from the shady bank,
no bright yellow petals and bells,

but in the yard of the man who has hated me for years,
who once coming down an aisle in a store
aimed his cart right at me, only veering at the end—
in the bark of his immaculate beds
groves of daffodils, forests of daffodils,
are exploding in all yellow and green profusion—

and at the house of the man
whose wife just died of ALS, unable to move, finally,
unable to breathe, but this happening slowly,
inexorably, day-by-day—her gnarling hand the last time
I gave her the Body of Christ canted sharply back
from her wrist, almost perpendicular—

on the edge of their sad and dreary lawn
the daffodils shine as yellow as the sun
a child might paint in school,

a lemony yellow sun,
smiling down on a Daddy and a Mommy
and a little girl.

Star

When you see someone you haven't seen in years,
and you hug and smile and start exchanging stories,
the mystery isn't that all the years have passed
but that they don't matter. You still love this person
the way you did before--his Irish jaw,
her Nebraska smile. You love them and care about
them the way you always did. And the next day
when morning comes with rain and it's fall and dark
and you walk in the rain and teach your classes
and eat your lunch alone in your office, you don't
think about them again, maybe once or twice,
a flash of pleasure and love, but you don't really think
about them again. The memory of them passes
from your mind as the memory of you has passed
from theirs, and you'll probably never think about them
again for more than a second or two, a quick image
of their faces, a sense of their bodies and their goodness.
In all the rest of your life, out of all the minutes
you have left and all the breaths, all the countless
thoughts you will have, they will be one tiny cell. One star.

The Sky Came Pouring Through

Most of the time we don't even realize
how judgmental we are. It's deep down.
The thick, creamy walls of the dormitory.
The wide, cool halls. But then the swallow
that came to the open window, hopping
on the sill. Ticking its dark, mechanical head.
This way. That way. I was hunched
over a desk, writing. My back was turned.
But I had that feeling you get when someone
is standing at your door, waiting for you
to turn around, and when I did, it didn't speak,
it flew away, and the freshness of the sky
came pouring through. The blue gulfs of air.

That Lonesome Whistle

Where I go in my head isn't an idea.

It's a place.

It's always there when I return,
with the same elements and the same
topography, like the hills
Jesus assuredly saw.

The way they vee down to the lake.

We know this.

The cups on the altar (again),
and some word in the Eucharistic Prayer (I can't remember which one),
and in the distance I hear the sound of a train.

A freight train, with boxcars, rattling over tracks
that come all the way from the Civil War.

First the bread is transformed, then we are. Then the world.

And I am both there, on that spot,
and somewhere else, on a periphery. In the past. Clickety-clacking.

Hear that lonesome whistle blow!

Puzzle

I used to think I was a boy in a family.
Then a hero in a story.
Then a voice, crying in the wilderness.
Now I am growing old,
and you and I are carrying a puzzle along a river.
The river runs through the city where we grew up,
strong and swift, and there are buildings on either bank,
some made of brick, with faded letters on the sides.
The puzzle is heavy—it has thousands of pieces—
and you and I keep passing the box back and forth,
taking turns carrying the weight of it.
We will need all winter to put it together,
poring over the pieces in the lamplight.
Outside the rain will fall. The wind will blow.
But inside, on the dining room table,
we will be building another city, piece by piece,
with a wavy blue river and a clean white church
and several ancient battlements,
and this one we will know by heart.

Our Trip to Spokane for a Wedding

I drive around town but don't remember where anything is.
My father is shrinking, he's getting smaller and smaller,
and he's losing his mind, too, I think. He says he gets in his car

and starts to drive but then can't remember where he's going,
and I'm no different. I keep making wrong turns, I keep getting lost,
and everything is changing anyway. Holy Cross
is now a daycare. The North Hill Public Library is a hair salon.

Driving back through the gorge I stop and climb to a waterfall.
There are hundreds of people on the paved path, and I resent them
at first, how fat they are and slow. But as we keep climbing

I start to join in the flow. All of our heads are bobbing, our arms
are swinging, and I think, the tall black man with the stiff knees
is my brother, the pretty little girl is me, and where else should we
be going but deeper and deeper into the shadows and the leaves?

At the top of the cliff we reach the waterfall, and the stream
is pouring over the edge, leaping and shining and scattering.
It's the Bridegroom! It's the Bridegroom, laughing!

Trust

Cresting the hill you see it,
above the fields and the tops of the walnut trees,
low in the sky, very close:
a giant hot air balloon, red and blue and green.

And there's a word spelled out on the side,
the letters tall as people: T-R-U-S-T.

You assume it's just advertising.
You think, there must be the name
of a bank on the other side.

But lately you've been so anxious. So afraid.

Long ago the Jews believed the Torah
was an orchard. From a distance all we see
are trees, but there are branches, too,
closer in, crissing and crossing,
and there are leaves, a profusion of leaves,
and there is the fruit in its many colors,
and the nuts in their many shells,
and beneath the skin the flesh,
and within the flesh the seeds.

And then you reach the bottom. Level out.
And the trees are wheeling past you,
the walnut trees, twisting and gnarled.
The rows are flashing by, one after the other,
the long, deep, darkening lanes.

A Thousand Pockets

I don't want to burst your
theological bubble, she said to me.

Yes, you do, I said.

It's taken me years to admit this.
A fine October afternoon,
leaves all the way to the library.

In the morning I walked in the forest
and watched how the sun picks out
the trunks of the trees one by one.

Loneliness is a craft,
Jack Gilbert says.

We have to learn how to live
with ourselves, among our thoughts.

The day has a thousand pockets.

Children's Hospital

Within a labyrinth of great buildings.
Early morning. The walkways still dark.
Smells of diesel and garbage. Already humid
and warm. Somewhere in a room you know
a little girl is dying, bald as an egg.
When she closes her eyes her eyelids flutter.
But it's so hard to care about other people.
To imagine what anyone else sees.
A shiny steel turbine. A tall, battered door.
In a courtyard a fountain, surrounded
by high walls. The air thick with the perfume
of flowers. The small, steady plume.

Ave Maria at the Crossing

Don't just talk about letting go.

There are *two* rivers:
the River of Forgetting,
and the River of Remembering.

A little bird will lead you,
rising and dipping in the air,
out past the trees.

There the water gleams like glass.
There the ferry brims with sheep.

Summer morning. Quiet. Dreamy.

Mary gazing over the gunwale,
not a thought in her head.

Density and Volume

As Dorinda lay dying there was fog
in the valley. Then sun.
Once it snowed. Then melted away.

But Dorinda was unaware.
Eyes closed. Breathing shallow.

In the summer, at Lisa and Greg's,
I looked through
Greg's telescope at the planet Mars.
It was a warm, velvet night.
And Mars wasn't red, it was yellow,
an ordinary, dirty yellow, and something
about that made me think:
Mars is a place, too. I thought:
we are both existing, at the same time.

Say there is a rock on Mars
in a shallow depression. That rock
has density and volume, and so do we.
That rock casts a shadow,
and so do we, and that shadow moves.

Walking down the long, bright hall.
Pushing on the half-open door.

But the bed is neatly made.
The sheets tucked in and smooth.
Pillow plumped. Crisp. White as snow.

Spring and Fall

In spring we wait
for the first yellow flash
of a warbler's wing.

In fall we wait
for the first yellow
turn of a leaf.

But the birds, of course,
are hiding, darting
in and out of the trees,

while now the leaves
they all have fallen,
and all the gray and

reaching branches
can be seen.

For His Name is Essence

Jerry Jenson was first-chair clarinet. I was second.
One of the things about him is that his father taught
accordion. Another is that he had no eyelashes.

None. He looked like a fish. Another is that every day
he'd go down to the field and practice place kicks,
one, two, three: kick; one, two, three: kick. Stiff-leg,

then follow through, looking up, again and again
and again, all seasons. Winter when the ground was slush
he'd bring a box of sawdust and keep working on form,

into the wind and rain and snow, every day, and finally,
game tied, seconds left, they put him in, and he made it,
the ball sailing high in the air, end over end, and in college

he walked on and fooled them again, still pear-shaped
and flatfooted, but now and then really connecting,
hard and clean, *one, two, three: kick.* And now I hear

he's the head coach at our old high school, pacing
the sidelines on Friday nights, handing out hats
at reunions. He laughs and smiles and pats your back,

blinking his lashless eyes. O why are you cast down,
my soul? Why groan within me? Hope in God;
I will praise him still, my savior and my God!

Smitty

Afternoons he'd poke his head through the gap
the open window made. His dark eyes
snapped. His spunky Van Dyke. He was waiting

for me to come home, he longed for me,
he lived for me. The white paint peeling from
the window frame. Our little house snug

as a cabin on a boat. 550 square feet. Beyond it
the wide gray water of the lake where
in the summer the voices clamored and the motors

lugged and surged, and then the mountains,
and the pass through the mountains.

That little dog still lives.

I tell you: that little dog still lives.

When Shy Ran Away

I was standing on the hill talking with a woman
who had stopped to say how much she loved
my book. A runner, young and lithe,
in a lithe group of runners, bouncy, neoprened,
and Shy, who had been nosing in the brambles
on the side of the road, was frightened,
I think. We'd only had him a week.

The woman was pressing her hands together
in an attitude of prayer, mock-bowing
but sincere, thanking me, when over her shoulder
I saw Shy burst from the brambles and shoot
down the road, flat out, ears flapping,
faster than I thought a little dog could run--
could fly: a small, black streak.

What I was wondering in the hours
I ran up and down the trail and back and forth
on the road, scanning the scrubby
February forest, every fallen branch a Yorkie mix,
was what might the nature of the revelation be
in a moment like this. What might it mean?

What did it mean that Shy was waiting for me,
on the front porch, trembling,
bedraggled, when I finally stumbled home?

Solitude and Gentleness

In a recording I heard of Thomas Merton lecturing
about peacefulness and prayer,
he talks fast and keeps saying see? see? at the end of sentences
like Edward G. Robinson in Little Caesar.

I'm going to get you, see? I'm going to make you pay, see?

Finally, they let him move into a cinderblock house in the woods
a mile or so from the monastery and the other monks.
At night as the stars blazed down he'd wake up and pee off the porch,
then go back inside and write in his journal. Pray the Vigil prayers.

For me it's always the morning stars
as I walk up the driveway for the paper.
Early September and already the sharpness in the air
and the wood smoke. The brilliant black sky. The stars, wheeling.

I just can't get over this.

The owl I hear hooting from somewhere in the trees
sounds just like a man blowing on a beer bottle.

A tall man, with a hat made of leaves.

Resemblances

It's funny how I kept thinking I saw Norma
after she died, on the edge of a crowd, disappearing
down a hall. Her silver hair. Her smoky lenses.

Or Dominic, from behind, with his round head
and hulking shoulders, turning left off the highway.

When a tree falls by the pond we see into the other stories.

A Barred Owl lifts from a branch, flapping hugely,
and settles on another, ruffled and indignant as a cat.
It stares at me whole seconds, unblinking.

In flight, the ragged leggings.

Everywhere I Am Received

I dive into the first of many rivers.
Swim across. Climb out. Hike to the next.

And some of these rivers are muddy and brown,
and some of them are silver and gold,
and some of them are so wondrously clear
I can see every pebble and fish.

Everywhere I am received, I am received.

Finally I arrive at the vineyard,
where I am sent to tend the vines. Calmly
I move among the lovely green rows,
binding and pruning, nibbling what is ripe.
Around me, all the others.

Driving the Dead Man's Truck

When I borrowed the keys to the dead man's truck,
I drove into town and ordered a sandwich.
Get out of here, he'd said, smiling kindly through
his snowy white beard. God that sandwich
tasted good, after all those silent days—the blandness
of the turkey against the sweetness of the bread.
God I loved driving that rusty old Toyota, rattling
down the shore. The endless ocean. The creamy waves.
There must be billions of miles on that engine.

This Ordinary Way

*with lines from David Foster Wallace
   and Karl Rahner*

Flinging fistfuls of Scott's Fall Turf Builder
with one gloved hand, holding the slick plastic bag
with the other, I walk through the yard
like the figure in the floppy hat in Van Gogh's
The Sower striding down the thick blue
furrows, a great orange and yellow sun rising up
behind him. Though it's misty and gray
and my yard is ringed with trees. The pellets
fly out in long lazy arcs. Irony tyrannizes.
Everything dies and everything rises
and this is how it really is. I do not lead a life.
I work and write and teach. I try to do my duty
and earn a living. I try this ordinary way
of serving God. Nitrogen and potassium and
all the other chemicals healing the dry,
desiccated roots. In spring the bright green grass.
Fluffy white clouds. The seed is the Word.

Lunch Hour

Some people have small heads
stuck on tall, spindly bodies.

Others seem to float, fluffy and light,
hoodies fresh from the dryer.

And all of them have hearts, and all of them have souls,
and through their eyes the Lord looks at the world he has made,
and with their hands he touches the world he has made,
and with their voices he sings of how much he loves it.

And my spirit begins to lift.
My sadness begins to ease.

And all this time I have been sitting on a bench
before a magnolia, and the leaves
of the magnolia have been scattering light,
and at the foot of the bench there has been a plaque
explaining who the bench was made
in loving memory of,
though it's not until I get up to go, brushing off
my pants, that I finally read the name.

It's the name of a woman I used to know,
upside down—
it's the name of a friend, and finally I see it,
embossed on the brass.

Crisply, like a commandment.

The Boy in the Bronco

blasts through a puddle on the street,
a lake, a pond, in the pouring-down rain,
a rusty Ford high above monster tires,
I glimpse a trucker cap, the water sheeting
up on either side like in the parting
of the Red Sea, and the wave on the far side,
an enormous wave, shoulder high,
breaking over a woman hurrying past,
head down, trying to get where she's going,

this much we know, can predict,

but not the stop, the sudden stop,
the boy in the Bronco coming to a halt
and leaning over and rolling down
the window and calling out his apology,
shouting over the rain--
or the woman laughing back, the woman
looking up and forgiving him, the water
streaming off her rain gear,
she is laughing, she is glistening,

I'm sorry I'm sorry I didn't know
you were there

Story

for Ted

You've got to promise not to bury me
next to that son-of-a-bitch,
she said, and years later when we finally did,
nestling their urns
into the same deep hole, hers and Dad's,
together again,
it began to rain. And not just rain:
it poured, and it hailed, and the wind came up
and inverted our umbrellas,
and we laughed and we laughed
as we sprinted toward our cars,
saying how pissed she was,
we've done it now!

though that was our hope, really,
our deepest desire,
that their lives and ours follow some kind
of pattern,
that we are in a story,
and the story never ends.

The Pentecost of Hands

When you bring your hands close together,
palms up, not touching, you may feel the *qi*
between them, the energy. This is what Joe says,
and I like Joe, his calm, deep voice,
his long lashes like a boy's. His smooth, bald head.
It's subtle, he says. You may not feel it
at first, but it's there. Use one hand as a laser pointer
and point at the other palm. Move in very slow
circles. Do you feel it? Or pull your hands
apart as if you are pulling apart a sticky dough,
then come back again. Sometimes in a circle
we hold our hands out to each other and close our eyes
and see what we can feel, and sometimes I think
I do feel something, very faint: maybe
just the tiny wind the hand makes when it moves,
or the heat the hand generates, the temperature
of the skin, and maybe this is the Holy Spirit, too,
why not? moving over the surfaces, or in them,
the Pentecost of Hands, the Pentecost of Skin
and the cells of the skin, that marvelous organ
that isn't just in one place like the other organs, located,
inside us, but stretching all over and conforming
to whatever shape the bones make. Think
of the hands of Jesus, holding a chunk of bread,
reaching out to raise up the old woman with the flu.
Palms up on the cross. Arms outstretched. Think
of my hands this morning as I gave the dogs their treat,
popping it into their mouths like communion.

What Knowing Really Means

I often feel as if I'm not really here.
But I am. I am no more

or less important than a wave
or a blade of grass or the crow

squawking in the top of that tree.
He obviously sees me.

I don't say *knows* me.

But what does *knowing* really mean
when our lives are so fleeting?

I crush the grass
and the grass closes over me.

I break the branch
and the forest closes over me.

How Happy I Am

On winter mornings in the dark
the small moss-covered branches of oak
and maple blown down by the wind
look just like the morning paper bundled
and tossed onto the wet driveway.
Different packets of information: lichen,
bark, the tiny insects the golden-crowned
kinglets forage for. DNA. Or in summer,
looking up at the open windows
of an old apartment building in Rome.
A woman leaning out with her sleeves
rolled up. Sunday morning. I can't believe
I'm really here, drinking cappuccino
at an outdoor table beneath a row
of tall, willowy trees. How happy I am.
I don't even know the language.

People Who Live by the Highway

People who live by the highway jangle and jump
at first. They can't sleep. I've heard the roar of traffic
compared to the roar of waves, but this isn't true.
Traffic is like thought. It's like the endless streaming
of your own hopes and fears, but that's just what you learn
to live with after a while. At night the semis shift up
and throttle out of town, and the SUV's never stop
whooshing by, but you open your windows anyway
and go to sleep, and you sleep like a baby.
Sometimes you make a cup of tea and sit outside
beneath the vast traffic of the stars, beneath the Milky Way,
which is moving, too, after all, at incredible speeds,
and you look out at the river of time as it goes flowing by,
and you smile. Because it's beautiful, it's a flowing
river of light, and it has nothing to do with you.

In Your Light We See Light

for Dick Allen

I watch moonlight fade through
the dark branches of trees on a winter morning.
Then darkness. Then sky again,
slowly brightening. This takes several minutes.

Like reading several poems by a man
the day after he died. I haven't read him before,
but yesterday he died, and now
I'm reading a poem he wrote about a cloud
no bigger than a man's hand, coming in off the sea,
and for a moment it takes my breath away.
I feel him talking to me. Then I go on with my day.

Up the street, on my neighbor's roof,
the giant inflatable Grinch has fallen over again,
facedown. But I can still see him
shining, red and white and green. Lit from within.

The Difference

for Barb

The difference between the sound
of the rain in winter
and the sound of the rain in spring
is the leaves,

is the sound of the rain falling
on all the countless
sheltering leaves,

is the difference
you make to me.

I Know Where This Goes

A scrap of spruce bark
exactly like a puzzle piece.

Two rounded edges
and a scoop.

I know where this goes.

A line of geese.
A burst of wind,

fanning the surface
of the bay.

Grateful acknowledgment is made to the editors of the publications where these poems first appeared:

Altarwork: "Trust"

Apple Valley Review: "The Neskowin Cottage Walk," "Christmas Letter," and "I Think I Hear the Cry of Geese"

Ascent: "A Blind Boy, on the Solstice"

Cortland Review: "Malta"

Literature Today: "A Question for the Stream"

Poetry Northwest: "Our Trip to Spokane for a Wedding"

Relief: A Journal of Art and Faith: "Transfigurations" and "You Never Know"

Verse Virtual: "So Long to Remember," "Liberty Says Hi," "Ephphatha," "When Shy Ran Away," "Solitude and Gentleness," and "In Your Light We See Light"

Windhover: "It Won't Be Long Now"

Sincere thanks

to Paul Willis, for his kindness and his counsel—without him, this book would not have been published;

to my colleague Karen Holmberg, for the lovely conversation we had;

to my friends Michael Milan, Lex Runciman, and Richard Wakefield, for their continued advice and support;

to Leah Browning, the editor of *The Apple Valley Review*, for her encouragement;

to Firestone Feinberg, the founder and editor of *Verse Virtual*, for his generosity of spirit;

to the fine poets who were kind enough to write blurbs: David Biespiel, Leah Browning, Scott Cairns, Joe Millar, and Paul Willis;

to James Janknegt, for permission to use his very striking painting, "Walking on Water," for the cover;

to Peter Betjemann, Director of the School of Writing, Literature, and Film at Oregon State University, and to the Smith Fund at Oregon State, for providing the funds to pay the permission fee for the cover;

to Kim Verhines, the director of Stephen F. Austin State University Press, for accepting the book in the first place;

and to Emily Townsend, my editor at SFASU Press and the book's designer as well, for her quickness and cheerfulness and skill.

photo by Maggie Kurniawan

Chris Anderson is a professor of English at Oregon State University in Corvallis, Oregon, and a Catholic deacon. He grew up in Spokane, Washington. He has published a number of books, both poetry and prose, most recently, *Light When It Comes: Trusting Joy, Facing Darkness, and Seeing God in Everything* (Eerdmans, 2016). He and his wife, Barb, live on the edge of the university research forest north of Corvallis with their two dogs, Pip and Shy. They have three children and two grandchildren.

For more about Chris, see www.deaconchrisanderson.com

CPSIA information can be obtained
at www.ICGtesting.com
Printed in the USA
LVHW04s0050250818
587829LV00003B/4/P